CW01512868

Original title:

Pallid Bends Across the Dragon Holm

Author: Olivia Orav

ISBN HARDBACK: 978-1-80562-998-6

ISBN PAPERBACK: 978-1-80564-519-1

Veiled Horizons Under Celestial Scales

In twilight's hush, the stars emerge,
Veiled secrets dance, a gentle surge.
Petals unfold in the silver mist,
Awakening dreams the night has kissed.

The moonlight guides with a tender hand,
Through shadowed trails of a forgotten land.
Each whispered breeze tells tales anew,
Of ancient hearts, both brave and true.

Clouds drift softly, like thoughts in flight,
Drawing constellations across the night.
Beneath the arch of the cosmic sea,
A spark ignites, setting spirits free.

In night's embrace, the world feels small,
Yet dreams expand, they beckon all.
Through veiled horizons, we'll wander wide,
With celestial scales as our trusted guide.

Whispering Ribbons Through the Languid Air

A ribbon of mist floats between the trees,
Carrying secrets upon a gentle breeze.
Soft voices echo, in whispers they share,
Tales of lost lovers and moonlit fare.

The languid air holds the warmth of sighs,
As shadows waltz beneath painted skies.
Memories flicker like fireflies bright,
Illuminating paths through the velvet night.

Each step we take is woven with grace,
In the heart of the forest, we find our place.
Whispering ribbons twining through fate,
Leading us onward before it's too late.

The dawn approaches with dreams to unfold,
Of magic held in the stories of old.
As we embrace the day's gentle breath,
We're woven together from life to death.

Distorted Lines of Timid Light

In the corridors where shadows creep,
Lines of timid light begin to leap.
Dancing echoes of forgotten days,
Fleeting figures in a world of haze.

Each flicker shimmers like a hidden thought,
Illuminating the battles we've fought.
Ghostly whispers weave through the gloom,
Echoing promises that once bloomed.

The labyrinth shifts with each breath we take,
A tapestry woven, where dreams awake.
Distorted lines guide us through the night,
To places where hope ignites our fright.

Each shadow painted with delicate ease,
Calls us to venture 'neath whispering trees.
Embrace the dance, let the darkness glide,
For within these lines, our spirits reside.

Shrouded Pathways Beneath the Winged Overpass

Beneath the arch where the shadows blend,
Shrouded pathways twist and bend.
Whispers of journeys long since passed,
Echo through time, their shadows cast.

The stars above weave stories of old,
In the silence where the night grows bold.
Each step we take on this hidden route,
Guided by instincts that shimmer and scout.

The scent of rain mingles with the dreams,
Flowing like rivers, or so it seems.
As winged wonders soar overhead,
We tread lightly where the brave have led.

Mysterious glimmers ignite the path wide,
Awakening courage we often hide.
With every breath, let our spirits rise,
Beneath the winged overpass of the skies.

Pale Streamers in the Serpent's Breath

Beneath the mist, the pale streamers glide,
Under the moon's watchful gaze they bide.
Whispers entwined in the night's cool air,
Lingering softly, with secrets to share.

Through twisting paths where shadows are cast,
The serpent stirs, its breath holds the past.
Silent sighs blend with the rustling leaves,
Ancient stories the darkness conceives.

In echoes of laughter, old spells ignite,
Woven by stars in the tapestry night.
Glistening softly, the streamers unfold,
Revealing the wonders that dreams dare to hold.

At dawn's embrace, the mist starts to wane,
Yet whispers linger, an enchanting refrain.
Pale streamers dissolve into morning light,
But echoes of magic still dance in the night.

Dull Currents of the Celestial Isle

In distant skies, where the dull currents sway,
The celestial isle meets the break of day.
Stars flicker softly, like lanterns in flight,
Guiding the dreamers who journey through night.

With every wave, there's a tale left untold,
Of wanderers brave, with hearts ever bold.
Beneath the shadows of emerald trees,
Whispers of wisdom ride on the breeze.

Through twilight's glow, the currents do weave,
Threads of fate, where the lost dare believe.
In quiet corners, the echoes entwine,
Drawing together the fates that align.

As daylight breaks, golden hues will ignite,
Awakening dreams that vanished from sight.
The isle remains, a sanctuary still,
In the heart of the wanderer's will.

Subtle Undulations in the Wyrm's Realm

In the depths of the wyrm's hidden domain,
Subtle undulations pulse softly like rain.
Rippling shadows, where secrets are kept,
Guarded by thrones where the ancients have wept.

With every flicker, the magic takes flight,
Whirling like stars in the heart of the night.
The wyrm's breath dances, a tender caress,
Embroidering time in a silken finesse.

Hidden beneath, where the mysteries gleam,
Whispers of dreams form a delicate seam.
Entwined in the flow, the past intertwines,
Echoing tales through the twisted designs.

As the night wanes, the shadows recede,
Leaving behind a soft, echoing creed.
In the wyrm's realm, where the lost may be found,
A circle of magic forever is bound.

Dimmed Glories of the Curving Tides

In the soft embrace of dimmed glories past,
The curving tides whisper, their shadows cast.
Memories linger in the salt of the foam,
Each wave a reminder of dreams left to roam.

Beneath the surface, where sorrows collide,
Echoes of laughter and heartaches reside.
In twilight's glow, the waters will sigh,
Glimmers of starlight that never say die.

Yet, in their depths, a quiet resolve,
A promise of hope that the hearts will evolve.
With each gentle pulse, the night brings a cure,
In the dance of the tides that shall ever endure.

As dawn breaks anew, with soft hues unfurled,
The curving tides cradle the dreams of the world.
In dimmed glories, the tales will align,
Reminding us all of the magic divine.

The Haunting Gaze of Slumbering Beasts

In the depths where shadows creep,
Rest the dreams and secrets deep.
Eyes like lanterns, dimmed and wise,
Guard the night with haunting sighs.

Silent whispers float on air,
Calling forth the brave to dare.
With each breath, the stillness breaks,
Beasts awaken from their wakes.

Glimmers of a dormant past,
Fade like echoes, slow and vast.
In the dark, their stories hum,
Spoken softly, yet so numb.

Tales of bravery long forgotten,
In the forest where hope's begotten.
With each rustle, a promise weaves,
In the hush, our heart believes.

Come, and listen to their cries,
As the moon adorns the skies.
In the gaze of slumbering beasts,
Lies the magic that never ceases.

Fables of the Twilight Realm

In the twilight where shadows play,
Fables dance at close of day.
Whispers echo through the trees,
Tales of wonders on the breeze.

Horizon kissed by softest gold,
Stories waiting to be told.
With each heartbeat, worlds collide,
In every crevice, secrets hide.

Creatures of the night arise,
Beneath the stars and silver skies.
Each flicker, each flutter, a sign,
Of the magic wrapped in time.

Elixirs brewed with starlit dew,
Bring forth dreams old yet anew.
In their dreams, our fears entwine,
Woven deeply with the divine.

So tread softly, heed your heart,
In this realm, we all take part.
For in fables, truth is spun,
While the twilight whispers run.

A Serpent's Tale Beneath the Veil

In the depths where shadows blend,
A serpent stirs, a tale to send.
Beneath the veil, the secrets coil,
Histories twisted, darkly royal.

Sleek and silent, thoughts entwine,
Winding paths of fate divine.
With every flick, a story's spun,
Of battles fought and races run.

Eyes like emeralds, fierce yet deep,
In their gaze, a promise keeps.
From legends lost in time's embrace,
The serpent weaves a timeless space.

Lurking where the shadows loom,
In every corner, fears find room.
Yet in the deep, a spark of light,
Guides the lost through endless night.

So heed the whispers from the dark,
They hold the key, ignite the spark.
In a serpent's tale, we find our way,
Beneath the veil, to learn and stay.

Harmonies of the Shimmering Shadows

When the twilight begins to sing,
Shadows dance on whispering wings.
In the silence, melodies weave,
Secrets heard, yet none believe.

Glistening echoes, soft and light,
Fill the air with magic bright.
Each note a fragment of a dream,
Flowing gently like a stream.

In the heart of the night's embrace,
Shadows gather, filling space.
Tales of yore, in whispers shared,
Echoes of those who truly dared.

Harmonies of twilight's glow,
Guide the lost through depths of woe.
In each tremor, hope revives,
In shimmering shadows, magic thrives.

So dance with shadows, heed their song,
In their rhythm, you belong.
For in this realm of softest sighs,
The heart finds truth that never dies.

Enigmas at the Edge of Dream

In shadows cast by whispering night,
Where secrets twine in silver light.
The stars unveil their hidden schemes,
As fantasies weave through tangled dreams.

Through veils of mist, the echoes play,
In realms where lost illusions sway.
Each thought a spark, each breath a song,
In this strange land where we belong.

A figure cloaked in moonlit grace,
Glides softly through this timeless space.
With every glance, the truth could gleam,
Yet shadows blur all we can deem.

A riddle rests upon the breeze,
Entwined with sighs of ancient trees.
The laughter of a distant child,
Hints at the magic, coy and mild.

Awake or sleep, which path is true?
In each reverie, a world anew.
With every breath, we chase the dawn,
Where enigmas wait, forever drawn.

The Canvas of Ethereal Hues

A brush dipped deep in twilight's glow,
Where colors dance and secrets flow.
With strokes of fate on canvas broad,
The universe reveals its odd.

In azure skies or emerald seas,
Where dreams are painted by the breeze.
Each hue a tale of hope and dread,
In shades where all desires tread.

The sun spills gold o'er hills of green,
As twilight whispers all unseen.
Reflections weave through every brush,
In this delightful, teasing hush.

From crimson hearts and shadows cast,
We craft a realm where spell is vast.
Each tick of time, a vibrant beat,
In artful dance, our lives repeat.

So place your heart upon the page,
And let it dream in vibrant sage.
With each stroke, the world will bloom,
In colors bright, dispelling gloom.

Lullabies of the Faded Realm

In twilight's grasp, where shadows sigh,
Soft lullabies of lost dreams fly.
They cradle hearts that dare to roam,
In suggestions of a long-lost home.

The air is thick with whispers faint,
Of stories penned by shimmering paint.
Each breath a note, each sound a plea,
Entwined in night's sweet mystery.

Where echoes haunt the silent glade,
And moonlit wishes gently fade.
A serenade of time long past,
In memory's arms, forever cast.

A melody of dreams once shared,
In fading light, a heart laid bare.
With every sigh, the past returns,
As fading embers softly burn.

So hush now, dear, let shadows play,
As lullabies will drift away.
In slumber's peace, may hope reside,
In the faded realm, where dreams abide.

Tides of Time in Ashen Waters

Beneath the moon's pale, wistful glow,
The tides of time begin to flow.
In waters deep and realms unknown,
A tale of ages lost is sown.

With every wave, a whisper calls,
As history's shadow gently falls.
Each ripple speaks of days once bright,
Enshrouded now in ambient night.

The heartbeats of the ages past,
Are echoes held in waves that cast.
From ash and stone, new paths arise,
While future dreams take to the skies.

In fracture's grace, where time conforms,
We find the beauty in the storms.
With memories like pearls, they gleam,
In ashen waters, we shall dream.

So sail the seas of what's gone by,
Where silence holds a thousand sighs.
In every tide, a promise waits,
Of time's embrace as fate dictates.

Ghostly Curves Through Wyrm's Lair

In twilight's hush, the shadows creep,
Through caverns deep, where secrets sleep,
With ghostly curves and whispers low,
The wyrm's dark heart begins to glow.

A flicker of scales, a glint of flame,
Echoes of glory, a forgotten name,
In the spiraled depths, dreams intertwine,
Haunting the air with tales divine.

Starlit whispers pierce the gloom,
A melody beckons from the ancient tomb,
Each step a dance on the dragon's breath,
Where stories fade, yet linger with death.

As shadows twist and shapes take flight,
Drawing forth wonders hidden from sight,
The past unfolds, a silken thread,
Weaving the fates of the lost and dead.

In ghostly curves, history weaves,
A tapestry formed from hopes and leaves,
Through wyrm's lair, where time stands still,
Echoing power, a haunting thrill.

Whispered Shadows of the Serpent's Pass

In the serpent's pass, where shadows drift,
Whispers of magic gently lift,
Through veils of mist, the secrets flow,
Churning the fate of all we know.

Beneath the stones, the echoes remain,
Soft sighs of those who felt the pain,
Each whispered word, a gift of the night,
Guiding the wanderers lost in their fright.

Gnarled branches stretch to the moonlit sky,
As silent spirits float gently by,
In every corner, a story unfurls,
Of ancient battles and forgotten worlds.

Treading softly on this hallowed ground,
Searching for solace, the lost have found,
In whispered shadows, truth intertwines,
The serpent's pass reveals its signs.

With every breeze, the magic sings,
From darkened caves to the heart of springs,
A realm where shadows play their part,
In the serpent's pass, they capture the heart.

Luminous Veils Over Ancient Scales

Beneath the yonder, where twilight glows,
Luminous veils in soft ebb and flows,
Draped upon scales of the ancient beast,
Guarding the secrets, a mythical feast.

Through pools of silver, reflections gleam,
An ocean of memories, a childhood dream,
Where past and present intertwine,
Illuminating shadows, so divine.

The dragon's breath, a gentle light,
Guiding the lost through the depth of night,
With every pulse, the magic swells,
In luminous veils, the heart compels.

A dance of colors, all intertwined,
Painting the tales of the brave and kind,
Each flicker speaks of adventures grand,
In luminous veils, forever they stand.

Ancient scales shimmer with tales of yore,
A treasure trove of forgotten lore,
Luminous veils in the dragon's keep,
Guardians of wisdom, where spirits leap.

Ethereal Twists in the Dragon's Embrace

In the dragon's hold, where shadows twine,
Ethereal twists in a dance divine,
Soft breath of fire, a warm caress,
Entwining fates in a world of excess.

Wings of dusk spread wide and free,
Carrying legends across the sea,
In spiraled dreams, the night takes flight,
Kissing the sky with stars so bright.

The heart of the beast, with secrets veiled,
Whispers of courage, love, and trails,
In the embrace, the stories unfold,
Of journeys traveled, of fortunes told.

As night drapes softly, the moon exclaims,
The power of dreams, the strength of names,
In ethereal twists, we all partake,
Crafting the destinies that we make.

In the dragon's embrace, we find our way,
Through echoes of night and the light of day,
Each moment cherished, each heartbeat grand,
In the timeless dance where spirits stand.

Veils of Time in the Ancient Hollow

In the hollow where whispers dwell,
The veils of time cast an ancient spell.
Shadows dance under the moon's soft light,
Carrying secrets of long-lost night.

Trees stand tall with stories to share,
Roots entwined in a delicate snare.
Echoes of laughter, a faint melody,
Bringing to life a forgotten reverie.

Leaves flutter gently, a soft sighing breeze,
Carving the essence of memories with ease.
Here, in the silence, the past comes alive,
Binding the present where dreams still thrive.

Candles flicker where shadows grow deep,
Guarding the silence, a promise to keep.
In this enchanted, serene, sacred glen,
Time bends and weaves through eternal again.

Glimmers of Hope amidst the Shadows

Amidst the shadows where night unfolds,
Glimmers of hope in the silence unfold.
Stars peer out from their velvet cocoon,
Painting the darkness with splashes of moon.

With each pulse of night, a whispering light,
Carries the promise of dawn's gentle flight.
Fleeting moments like fireflies bright,
Chasing away whispers of impending night.

In the heart of despair, where doubts conspire,
Glimmers ignite like a spark from a fire.
Hold on to dreams, let your spirit arise,
For in that darkness, the bravest light lies.

Through treacherous paths, as shadows grow long,
The music of hope plays a soft, vibrant song.
Rise from the ashes, let your spirit soar,
For glimmers of hope will forever restore.

Mysteries in the Dusk's Embrace

In the cradle of dusk, when day meets the night,
Mysteries weave through the fading light.
Veils of twilight cloak the world in dreams,
Beyond the horizon, reality seems.

Footsteps echo on the soft, cool ground,
Secrets whispered, yet never found.
Stars begin to wink in a playful dance,
Inviting the heart to take a chance.

The sky blushes softly, a painter's caress,
Time pauses gently, inviting us to rest.
In shadows that linger, stories unfold,
Of love everlasting and destinies bold.

Wrapped in the night, a soft breath away,
Mysteries linger, come what may.
The dusk holds a magic that deepens the hue,
Where dreams take flight, finding paths anew.

A Wraith's Serenade at Sundown

As the sun dips low beneath the tall pines,
A wraith sings softly, threading sweet lines.
With a voice like the wind, it dances through air,
Summoning echoes of tender despair.

The twilight reveals specters lost in their song,
Mourning and joy, their sorrows prolong.
In the fading light, memories drift,
A haunting serenade, a spectral gift.

Crickets are chiming their nightingales' tune,
While fireflies twinkle beneath a bright moon.
Each note tells a story of love's sweet refrain,
Borne on the breath of a whispering rain.

As shadows deepen, the wraith softly sighs,
Adrift in the stillness, where the heart learns to rise.
In the closing of day, as dreams intertwine,
You'll hear the serenade that echoes divine.

Whispers of a Faded Horizon

In twilight's glow, where secrets lie,
Dreams cascade across the sky.
The whispers dance on a gentle breeze,
Telling tales of forgotten trees.

Beneath the arch of a silver arch,
Time wanders, slow, on a tranquil march.
With every breath, the past unfolds,
Casting shadows where magic holds.

Stars awaken in the velvet night,
Guiding hearts with their tender light.
In their gleam, hopes rise anew,
Faded horizons beckon too.

The moon hangs low, a watchful eye,
Guarding dreams that dare to fly.
In silence, wishes softly bloom,
Carving paths through the darkening gloom.

As dawn arrives, the light will spill,
Awakening the world, silent and still.
With every dawn, the whispers fade,
Yet in our hearts, the magic's laid.

Shadows in the Glistening Mist

In the hush of twilight, shadows creep,
Veiling whispers while the world sleeps.
The mist enfolds like a silken shroud,
Where dreams wander, daring and proud.

Silver droplets cling to leaves,
A symphony spun from the night that weaves.
In the hush, secrets softly gleam,
Fragments of an ethereal dream.

Mystic shapes in the vapor dance,
Calling forth the night's romance.
With every turn, the shadows swirl,
In their embrace, the lights unfurl.

Among the echoes, a soft sigh,
Of hopes that linger and dare to fly.
In the glistening mist, we find our way,
As dawn prepares to claim the day.

So let the shadows spin their tale,
A tapestry where dreams set sail.
Bound by whispers, we weave our course,
In the mist, we find our force.

Echoes of Enchanted Valleys

In valleys wrapped by time's embrace,
Echoes linger, soft as lace.
The breeze carries secrets long untold,
In whispers of magic, brave and bold.

Sunlight bathes the hills in gold,
Awakening stories of the old.
Where laughter mingles with the stream,
And echoes awaken a slumbering dream.

Petals fall like gentle tears,
Each a memory of bygone years.
Among the flowers, the past shall rise,
In the cradle of time, under azure skies.

The chorus sings of joy and pain,
In enchanted valleys, hope retains.
With every rustle, hearts align,
Writing stories in this sacred shrine.

As twilight deepens, shadows play,
Filling the air with their soft ballet.
In this haven, we gather near,
For echoes of love are always clear.

The Gloom of Celestial Currents

In the depths where shadows weave,
Celestial currents whisper and cleave.
A solemn hush blankets the night,
Where stars falter in their flight.

The sky, a canvas of deepening blue,
Holds secrets painted in every hue.
Twinkling eyes hide tales of old,
In their depths, the mysteries unfold.

Beneath the weight of the endless dome,
Lost souls wander, far from home.
In their hearts, a longing song,
Echoing softly where dreams belong.

The nightingale sings of faded grace,
As shadows dart in this haunted space.
With every note, the gloom expands,
Binding together our trembling hands.

Yet in the darkness, hope remains,
Carved in the love of unseen chains.
Through celestial currents, we shall rise,
Finding light in the starlit skies.

Ghostly Reflections on Still Waters

In the twilight's hush, shadows stir,
Soft whispers gliding, secrets blur.
Mirrors of moonlight, silver lace,
Ghostly visions in still waters' embrace.

Ripples dance where dreams do tread,
Echoes of lives that once were wed.
Forgotten faces, tales of sorrow,
In every gleam, a lost tomorrow.

Winds carry tales of old regret,
Among the reeds, their shadows met.
Silent cries beneath the sky,
As we look, the echoes sigh.

Beneath the surface, time stands still,
Hearts entwined with an iron will.
The lake reflects our deepest fears,
In ghostly splendor, we shed our tears.

As night unfolds, the spirits wane,
Guided by stars, they break their chain.
In stillness found, their stories wake,
On ghostly tides, the past we stake.

The Song of Wandering Spirits

Through twilight's veil, they softly tread,
Wandering souls, where dreams are fed.
With every sigh, a tale is spun,
In ancient woods, their journey's begun.

The wind sings low, a haunting tune,
Carrying whispers, under the moon.
In shadows deep, their laughter plays,
A melody lost in forgotten days.

With flickering lights, their memory gleams,
In twilit hours, they dance in dreams.
Across the glen, in soft embrace,
Wandering spirits find their place.

Beneath the boughs, in night's sweet breath,
They weave through time, in life and death.
In echoes soft, their stories blend,
The song of spirits that never end.

A flicker of light, a fleeting glance,
In every step, a ghostly dance.
So listen close, and you may find,
The song of wandering, forever entwined.

Echoes from the Wyrm's Nest

In caverns deep, where shadows loom,
Wyrms whisper secrets, and dangers bloom.
Through ancient stone, their stories seep,
In the heart of the darkness, old fears creep.

Scales like armor, glinting bright,
Guarding the treasures shunned by light.
Echoes of battles long since fought,
In the nest of the wyrm, wisdom is sought.

Fiery breath, a warning's call,
In stillness caught, we heed their thrall.
The rustle of wings, a shuddering sound,
In the lair of the wyrm, legends abound.

Golden gems and silver threads,
Looming shadows where no one treads.
The whispers grow, and fate draws near,
In the echoes of time, we face our fear.

Yet within the depths, a light shines through,
Guarded by wyrms, both fierce and true.
In shadows cast, the brave shall quest,
To claim the fate from the wyrm's nest.

Beneath the Veil of Forgotten Legends

In the folds of time, where legends sleep,
Lies a tapestry rich, in secrets deep.
Whispers of ages lost in the haze,
Beneath the veil, the past betrays.

Faded ink on brittle page,
Tales of valor, love, and rage.
When shadows gather and daylight wanes,
The stories echo through blood and veins.

From heroes bold to villains sly,
In each heartbeat, their spirits lie.
A flicker of hope against the night,
Beneath the veil, there shines a light.

Ancient oaks guard the silent lore,
Of battles fought and friendships pure.
As the moon casts its soft embrace,
Forgotten legends find their place.

So linger here, where tales unfold,
In whispered tones, they beckon bold.
Beneath the veil of what's unknown,
The spirit lives, forever grown.

Nostalgia in Autumn's Veil

Leaves flutter down like whispers,
Embracing earth in golden hues.
Each step echoes with memories,
In the crisp air, the past imbues.

The sun dips low, a painted glow,
Casting shadows that dance and play.
Time wraps gently around my heart,
As autumn sings its soft ballet.

Rustling trees tell tales of old,
In secrets held by twilight skies.
The warmth of laughter lingers close,
As the chill of time softly sighs.

Firelight crackles, shadows flicker,
In the hearth, stories warm my soul.
With each ember, a memory stirs,
In the chaos, I find my whole.

Embrace the dusk, let it unfold,
In its arms, let worries cease.
For in the autumn's grand embrace,
Lies a moment of perfect peace.

The Harmony of Dimmed Colors

In twilight's soft and muted light,
The world transforms, a quiet sigh.
Brushstrokes of dusk blend into night,
Painting dreams in the evening sky.

Whispers of brown and gold unfold,
Nature's palette, serene and sweet.
Each hue a thread in tales retold,
In the silence, past and present meet.

Crickets serenade the cool breeze,
While stars awaken, blinking bright.
As harmony wraps around the trees,
The canvas of life ignites the night.

Fleeting moments float like leaves,
Suspended in the evening's glow.
With every breath, the heart believes,
That beauty lies in ebb and flow.

Let the darkness cradle hope,
In the stillness, dreams begin.
For in this dance, we learn to cope,
Finding warmth where we have been.

Strands of Memory in the Mist

Morning fog drapes the world in white,
As secrets linger, soft and shy.
Each breath a cloud, each step a flight,
In the shroud, lost echoes lie.

Worn paths weave through the tangled trees,
Where whispers once dared to tread anew.
Time unravels like a gentle breeze,
Uncovering dreams long overdue.

With every shadow that flits past,
A story finds its voice to say.
In the haze, the echoes hold fast,
Revealing colors of yesterday.

Stillness wraps around like a shawl,
Embracing memory's tender kiss.
In the quiet, I hear the call,
Of all the moments I can't miss.

So let the mist be my guide today,
Leading me through the shades of lore.
For in its depths, I find my way,
Homeward to places I adore.

The Soul's Journey beyond the Veil

With gentle hands, the night draws close,
A veil of stars to guide my flight.
Through realms unknown, my spirit goes,
Where dreams dance freely in the night.

Each heartbeat pulses, a rhythmic song,
As shadows whisper of paths entwined.
In the silence, I know I belong,
To places only my heart can find.

The moonlit tide pulls between worlds,
An ebb and flow of timeless grace.
In this moment, the universe swirls,
A glimpse of hope, a fleeting trace.

Stepping softly, I embrace the thin,
The veil that separates the past.
With every breath, I let love in,
And weave the futures meant to last.

In the embrace of the twilight sky,
The journey's essence wraps me whole.
I let the stars teach me to fly,
As I discover the depths of soul.

Shadows Dance on the Moonlit Isle

Soft whispers glide through trees,
While midnight's cloak enfolds the ground.
A silver orb hangs high with ease,
As secrets in the dark abound.

Reflecting tales of long ago,
Where dreams and nightmares intertwine.
The shadows twist, begin to flow,
Creating scenes both dark and fine.

With every rustle in the leaves,
The night reveals a hidden path.
Where magic stirs and hope believes,
Their dance ignites a spellbound wrath.

The waves caress the sandy shore,
As starlight twinkles in the sea.
Each moment teems with ancient lore,
Inviting hearts to wander free.

Yet caution treads on silent feet,
For glimmers hide what's not in sight.
In shadows deep, the unknown greets,
Ensnaring souls 'neath pale moonlight.

Ethereal Rays through the Gloom

Faint glimmers pierce the shrouded sky,
As dawn unfurls her golden hue.
The shadows wane, yet sigh and lie,
Whispering tales of darker view.

Through misty veils, the sun breaks clear,
While darkness bends beneath her reign.
Each beam of light, a muse so dear,
A promise wrapped in joy and pain.

Glimpses of hope emerge anew,
As fears retreat to hidden nooks.
The ethereal calls, both sweet and true,
While nature's pulse in silence crooks.

With every ray, courage ignites,
Awakening the world once more.
Through shadows past, the heart ignites,
And whispers dreams we can explore.

Yet darkness lingers, never far,
Its grip a stark, enduring sway.
We chase the light; we bear the scar,
And seek the dawn, come what may.

Hushed Footsteps in the Mist

In corners where the shadows creep,
A silken hush blankets the ground.
Each step a secret meant to keep,
In twilight's breath, no voice is found.

The veil of fog begins to swirl,
As echoes call from deep within.
A magical dance begins to twirl,
Ensnared in silence, we spin.

Where trees stand tall, their whispers faint,
And branches weave a shrouded nest.
The quiet grows, though hearts may taint,
With longing thoughts that never rest.

Each footstep tells a tale unsaid,
Of wanderers lost in their plight.
And as they tread, a thread is spread,
Binding them to the cloak of night.

So tread with care, dear souls who roam,
For every path leads to a choice.
In misty shrouds, we find our home,
With hushed footsteps, we embrace the voice.

Lament of the Lurking Beasts

Beneath the moon's pale, watchful eye,
Where wild things stir, their spirits snare.
A mournful howl fills up the sky,
A call for kin, a deep despair.

With eyes like embers quick and bright,
The lurking beasts prowl through the night.
They hold the tales of ages past,
In shadows deep, their memories cast.

Echoes of loss and battles fought,
Resound among the twilight trees.
The primal pulse of nature caught,
In whispered winds, the chilling breeze.

They mourn the trails long left behind,
Of kinship forged in twilight's gleam.
No comfort found, no peace of mind,
Their lament flows in the silver stream.

Yet in their night, a grace remains,
A bond unbroken, fierce and true.
Through shadows dark and hidden gains,
The lurkers roam while skies renew.

Murmurs of Ancient Seasons

In whispers soft, the leaves do sway,
With tales of yore and the light of day.
The sun will rise, the shadows fall,
As ancient stories begin to call.

The autumn breeze carries scents of gold,
A hint of magic in the air so bold.
Spring will dance with blooms anew,
While winter weaves its blanket of blue.

The summer's laughter fills the glade,
Where memories of warmth shall never fade.
Each season's hands gently intertwine,
A tapestry of moments, pure and fine.

So listen close, let nature sing,
Of cycles vast and the joy they bring.
In every seed and every breeze,
Murmurs of ancient seasons tease.

Upon the canvas, time takes flight,
Each brushstroke kissed by day and night.
In every heart, a story starts,
Of ancient seasons, whispered arts.

The Tapestry of Thorns and Twilight

Beyond the dusk, where shadows creep,
A tale is woven, in silence deep.
Thorns entwine with petals fair,
A tapestry spun from dreams laid bare.

In twilight's embrace, the stars ignite,
A canvas of wonders, shadow and light.
Each thread a whisper, a forgotten name,
In the fabric of night, we play our game.

The winds of change sigh soft and low,
As secrets of thorns begin to flow.
An endless dance of joy and pain,
Where love and loss both stake their claim.

Hidden truths in darkness dwell,
In every heartbeats, a silent bell.
The tapestry glimmers, rich and grand,
A story of thorns, by twilight's hand.

So cast your gaze on the evening's crown,
Where dreams awaken, and fears drown.
In the twilight's hush, let beauty take flight,
Within the tapestry, both dark and bright.

Chronicles of the Hidden Pass

Through misty veils, where legends roam,
A hidden pass calls my heart to home.
With every step, the past draws near,
And echoes of old whisper in my ear.

A winding path through ancient trees,
Where secrets linger on the breeze.
Footprints of time, both bright and dim,
In shadows deep, I dance with whim.

The stories rise from earth and stone,
Chronicles written in a language known.
The rustling leaves, the murmurs loud,
Guide me through the haunting crowd.

Every corner turned, a tale unfolds,
Of brave hearts, and treasures untold.
In the hidden pass, adventure waits,
As fate weaves tales beyond the gates.

So journey forth, let courage blaze,
In the chronicles, I'm lost, amazed.
For in every step, my spirit flies,
Through the hidden pass, my heart replies.

The Daunting Beauty of Fleeting Time

In twilight's glow, the past takes flight,
A dance of shadows, fading light.
Time, a river, swift and bright,
With stories penned beneath the night.

Each moment precious, a shimmering spark,
Fleeting whispers in the dark.
The seasons shift, yet memories climb,
The daunting beauty of fleeting time.

Like petals drifting on the breeze,
We seek to hold what cannot seize.
Yet in the chase, we find our grace,
In every heartbeat, in every space.

For life is but a fragile thread,
A tapestry where dreams are spread.
In laughter's echo, and in sorrow's chime,
We learn to cherish the fleeting time.

So raise a glass to those we find,
Within the beauty, and peace of mind.
For though it fades, love's light will shine,
In the daunting beauty of fleeting time.

The Fluttering Wings of Nightfall

As shadows stretch and darkness blooms,
The fluttering wings hum haunting tunes.
In twilight's grasp, the secrets rise,
Wrapped in whispers, beneath the skies.

The stars emerge with gentle grace,
Illuminating the night's embrace.
A world where dreams and wishes play,
In the stillness of the fading day.

The soft caress of moonlit beams,
Entwined within our quiet dreams.
Night creatures stir, their eyes aglow,
In this realm where magic flows.

With every flap, a tale unfolds,
Of ages past and futures bold.
The fluttering wings in the dark skies,
Guide lost souls with their gentle sighs.

So let us wander, hand in hand,
Into the night, a promised land.
As the fluttering wings take flight,
We'll dance beneath the stars tonight.

Whispers in the Murky Woodlands

In the depths where shadows dwell,
A haunting song, the trees do tell.
Whispers float on the crisp night air,
Secrets held with utmost care.

Branches sway with a spectral grace,
Guardians of this hidden place.
Footsteps echo, then softly fade,
Lost in dreams that time has made.

A nightingale calls, its voice so clear,
Echoes of past, drawing near.
Among the roots, the faeries play,
In moonlit glades, where magic stays.

Misty veils shroud the ancient trees,
Weaving tales on the gentle breeze.
Each rustle hints at stories spun,
Of dusk until the rise of sun.

So wander deep, where legends lie,
In murky woodlands, beneath the sky.
For every whisper, a spark ignites,
In the heart of these enchanted nights.

The Art of Embracing the Unseen

In shadows cast where visions dwell,
The art of seeing, none can tell.
With open hearts, and spirits free,
We find the truths that cannot be.

Invisible lines that bind our fate,
In the quiet space, we patiently wait.
For every glance and fleeting thought,
Holds the magic that time forgot.

The unseen weave through every thread,
In whispered dreams that dance in our head.
Embrace the silence, let it speak,
For in stillness, we are made unique.

A spark ignites, a fleeting sign,
The universe in twinkling design.
Through veils of doubt, we seek the light,
Finding wonder in shadowed night.

So let us hold the unseen close,
With every heartbeat, let us boast.
For in the art of love and dreams,
Life unfolds in shimmering beams.

Silhouettes in the Sacred Mist

In the mist where shadows blend,
Silhouettes of dreams ascend.
Softly gliding, they twist and turn,
In sacred folds, we yearn and learn.

The rising fog, a gentle shroud,
Secrets known to the silent crowd.
Each figure whispers stories past,
In fleeting glimpses, shadows cast.

We wander through this hallowed air,
Finding beauty hidden, rare.
As the fog drifts with tender grace,
We glimpse the echoes in their place.

An ancient dance, the spirit's sway,
In soft-lit realms where lost dreams play.
A tapestry of life entwined,
In silhouettes, our truths we find.

So take my hand, we'll trace the night,
Through swirling mist and fading light.
For in this sacred, whispered breeze,
Our hearts are free, our souls at ease.

Dances with Faint Spirits

In the twilight's gentle sway,
Where shadows whisper low,
Faint spirits begin to play,
In the moon's soft, silver glow.

They twirl upon the misty ground,
With laughter like a breeze,
A melody that knows no bound,
Entwined with ancient trees.

Each step a tale of yore,
Of dreams and fleeting light,
As they glide forevermore,
In the hush of the night.

Their eyes hold secrets vast,
Of worlds beyond our own,
In dances that forever last,
Where the heart feels less alone.

So join this spectral rite,
Let worries fade away,
In the beauty of the night,
Let the spirits guide your play.

Glimpses of a Forgotten Dream

Amidst the haze of morning mist,
Lies a dream once held dear,
Fleeting echoes in the twist,
Of time that disappears.

Whispers of a vibrant past,
In corners of the mind,
Illusions that forever last,
What treasures once could find.

The sun breaks through the gloom,
Casting shadows of the old,
Awakening a silent bloom,
In stories yet untold.

Each sigh a breath from long ago,
A reflection of the soul,
In the sunlight's golden glow,
We journey to be whole.

So open up your heart and see,
The dreams that still may soar,
In every glance, a memory,
A life just waiting for more.

The Tempest's Embrace that Never Was

In the stillness before the storm,
Where hopes begin to rise,
A tempest waits to take its form,
Beneath the darkened skies.

Clouds gather with a restless sigh,
As the winds begin to howl,
Yet still the heart dares not to cry,
For fears in stillness prowl.

Each flash of lightning holds a spark,
Of dreams that might ignite,
In shadows deep, where none embark,
To face the brewing night.

But with the roar, the soul must learn,
To dance within the squall,
For in adversity, we yearn,
To rise, to stand, to call.

So let the tempest come today,
Let winds of change embrace,
In every storm, we find the way,
To navigate with grace.

Journeying through the Enigmatic Wilds

In the woods where shadows blend,
With secrets deeply sewn,
A journey starts that few might end,
To wander there alone.

The winding paths, they twist and weave,
Through canopies of green,
With whispers calling, hard to believe,
In places rarely seen.

Each rustle brings a tale anew,
Of creatures wide and wise,
In the heart of wilds so true,
Beneath the watchful skies.

As the dawn breaks over hills,
With colors bright and bold,
The spirit of adventure spills,
In wonders to behold.

So step into this sacred space,
Where nature takes her stand,
And find your heart's most needed place,
In the wild's gentle hand.

Murmurs from the Eldritch Shadows

In the depths where shadows play,
Strange voices rise with night's decay.
Whispers weave through ancient trees,
Secrets carried on the breeze.

Moonlit paths and restless sighs,
Lurking truths in dark disguise.
Through brambles thick and spirits lost,
What is gained and what the cost?

Echoes dance in twilight's grip,
Cloaked in mist, the phantoms slip.
Every rustle brings a tale,
Of forgotten worlds, frail and pale.

Stars above like watchful eyes,
Guard the tales of where it lies.
Murmurs call, a summons sweet,
Adventurers rise, their hearts repeat.

So venture forth, brave hearts aglow,
Into shadows, soft and slow.
For where light fades, new paths ignite,
In the dark, the magic's light.

The Quiet Melancholy of Dusk

As daylight bows to winding night,
The skies embrace a softer light.
A hush descends, a tender sigh,
The sun bids farewell, saying goodbye.

Crimson hues on restless waves,
Whispers of time that gently paves.
Each moment lingers, bittersweet,
In twilight's glow, our hearts retreat.

Shadows stretch with graceful ease,
A quiet dance in evening's breeze.
Beneath the stars, our dreams unfold,
In the silence, stories told.

The world is painted in shades of blue,
A canvas vast, a tranquil hue.
With every heartbeat, memories play,
In the fading light of day.

A soft lament, a whispered prayer,
For the moments lost, laid bare.
Embrace the dusk, let sorrow blend,
For night shall come, but never end.

A Journey through Whispering Valleys

Through valleys deep where shadows sing,
The echoes call with every wing.
Glimmers in the dappled light,
Lead us forth into the night.

Footfalls soft on emerald grass,
Time is fleeting, moments pass.
Starlit skies above us twirl,
In the breeze, our dreams unfurl.

Mountains loom like giants old,
Guardians of the tales retold.
Step by step, the path we trace,
In this land, there's endless grace.

Roots entwined in gentle embrace,
Guide our hearts to a sacred place.
Where stories linger in thin air,
An adventure waits, beyond compare.

So let us wander, hand in hand,
Through whispering hopes in this enchanted land.
For every valley holds a key,
To secrets whispered, wild and free.

The Tempest's Softening Grasp

When storms rattle the heavens high,
And thunder rumbles, darkened sky.
Yet in the chaos, hearts collide,
Finding solace, side by side.

Winds that howl through open fields,
Nature's fury, a shield that yields.
Beneath the clouds, our spirits rise,
In the tempest's dance, we realize.

Raindrops like whispers, sweet and clear,
Soothe the soul, wash away fear.
With every flash, a moment bright,
Guiding us through the darkest night.

Time may crumble, yet still we stand,
Together forging a life, so grand.
Through every storm, we'll find our way,
In the softening grasp of the day.

So let the tempest swirl and thrash,
For love will bloom, no matter the clash.
In the eye of the storm, we'll embrace,
The beauty of chaos, wrapped in grace.

The Hallowed Grounds of Legend

In shadows deep where secrets lie,
The whispers of the past drift by.
Forgotten paths of ancient lore,
In every stone, a tale of yore.

Beneath the boughs of time-worn trees,
The winds tell stories with gentle ease.
Where heroes trod with hearts so bold,
Their echoes linger, bright as gold.

The moonlit glade, a sacred place,
Where dreams entwine in soft embrace.
The spirits dance in twilight's glow,
While fireflies weave their quest below.

With every step, a chance to find,
The threads of fate, so intertwined.
In hallowed grounds, their legacies,
Shall bind the lost with memories.

So heed the call of whispered sighs,
For in their depths, true magic lies.
The past and present, hand in hand,
Awaken dreams in this enchanted land.

Sorrowful Tales Beneath the Stars

Upon the canvas of the night,
Tales of sorrow find their flight.
Stars like tears, they softly gleam,
As shadows weave a fragile dream.

Each twinkle speaks of hearts once whole,
Of whispered hopes and lost control.
The moon reflects a silver sheen,
A haunting glow on worlds unseen.

Beneath the vast, celestial sea,
The stories whisper, wild and free.
In every star, a midnight tear,
A testament to love and fear.

But amongst the pain, the light does creep,
Awakening dreams from sorrow's sleep.
For every tale of loss that's spun,
A thread of hope begins to run.

So gaze above, and learn to find,
The beauty in the ties that bind.
For under stars, we'll ever share,
The tender echoes of despair.

The Lament of the Lost Horizon

Beyond the peaks where shadows creep,
A horizon lost in silence deep.
The sun descends, a fleeting fire,
Its colors fade, a soft desire.

In whispered winds, the echoes sigh,
Of dreams forsaken, left to die.
Yet once they shimmered, bold and bright,
Now memories fade into the night.

The valleys hum with tales untold,
Of wanderers dreaming to be bold.
Each step a wish upon the breeze,
To find the dawn amidst the trees.

But time, it steals what hearts hold dear,
The laughter lost, the muted cheer.
As mountains rise, so do our fears,
A tale of longing through the years.

Yet in the dusk, a glimmer stays,
A promise woven through the haze.
For every horizon, dark and wide,
Leads to a place where dreams abide.

Reveries in the Graying Light

As daylight wanes, the shadows blend,
In reveries where thoughts ascend.
The graying light, a tender shroud,
Embraces whispers, soft and loud.

In quiet moments, dreams take flight,
And dance upon the cusp of night.
With every sigh, a tale unfolds,
Of secrets shared and hopes retold.

The fading sun, a painter's brush,
Leaves strokes of gold in twilight's hush.
In every shadow, stories play,
A symphony of dusk and day.

Yet in this twilight's gentle phase,
The world's enchantment starts to blaze.
For in the graying, magic stirs,
As night blooms forth with whispered purrs.

So linger long where twilight glows,
And honor all the dreams that rose.
In reveries, our spirits soar,
Through graying light forevermore.

Fading Echoes of a Lost Skyline

Upon the dusk, the shadows fall,
Whispers of stars, a distant call.
Once bright dreams now softly sigh,
In twilight's arms, the memories lie.

Veiled in mist, the rooftops fade,
Echoes of laughter softly played.
A canvas once of vibrant hue,
Now painted gray, the sky anew.

The lights that danced, now one by one,
Flicker like tales that come undone.
In the quiet, a secret's kept,
Of all the things we dared to dream and wept.

As twilight breathes its final grace,
Time's gentle hand begins to trace.
Each fading echo, a whispered token,
Of hopes once bright, now softly broken.

Yet in the dark, a spark remains,
A promise woven through the pains.
For in the night, we find our way,
Through fading echoes that softly play.

Misty Paths Beneath the Shimmering Wing

In twilight's hush, the whispers glide,
Misty paths where dreams reside.
Beneath the wings of shadows cast,
We wander forth, hearts beating fast.

The air is thick with secrets old,
Stories waiting to be told.
Each step a dance, a fleeting chance,
Awakening hope in a dreamlike trance.

Stars below in twilight's seam,
Guide us gently, a silver beam.
Through tangled woods and shimmering light,
We chase the shadows of the night.

In silence deep, the world unwinds,
Lost in magic, our fates entwined.
As whispers rise on the crisp, cool air,
We find our purpose, our souls laid bare.

Each path we tread, a story spun,
Beneath the gaze of the ancient sun.
Together we forge the way anew,
On misty paths, our dreams come true.

Chilling Lines of the Enchanted Fold

In the folds of twilight, shadows creep,
Where ancient secrets dare to sleep.
A chilling breeze through branches calls,
As twilight dances and darkness falls.

Whispers weave through the haunted glade,
Stories of love that never stayed.
Each haunting note a memory spun,
Of dreams lost beneath the dying sun.

The trees stand tall, their limbs entwined,
Guardians of tales that time confined.
A shiver runs down the spine of night,
As echoes whisper of forgotten light.

In every sigh, the past resides,
Magic stirs where the forest hides.
Chilling lines, a tapestry bold,
Of lives once lived and legends told.

A flicker of hope in shadows' hold,
Awakens dreams, as the night grows cold.
In enchanted folds, we shall explore,
The heart of magic forever more.

Haunting Silhouettes Through the Wyvern Vale

In the vale where the wyverns soar,
Haunting silhouettes, tales of yore.
Beneath the moon's attentive gaze,
We wander through the spectral haze.

Whispers travel on the sighing breeze,
Tales of magic that aim to please.
Each shadow cast, a story told,
Of brave hearts and treasures bold.

The ground is rich with ancient lore,
As twilight's shroud begins to pour.
Through glens of dark and silver streams,
Life intertwines with our wildest dreams.

In every rustle, the past awakes,
Jumping from deep where silence shakes.
With wide-eyed wonder, we chase the night,
Toward figures dancing in soft moonlight.

In Wyvern Vale, we heed the call,
To explore the magic that binds us all.
Haunting silhouettes guide our way,
Through the tapestry of night and day.

The Last Sigh of the Wakened Isle

Upon the shores where shadows dwell,
The last sigh whispers, like a spell.
Waves cradle dreams on softest sands,
While time drifts lightly through our hands.

The dawn unveils a secret light,
Painting the sky in hues of bright.
Each cresting wave a tale unfurled,
Of forgotten love in a waking world.

Birds take flight with joyous cries,
Chasing wonders through endless skies.
The island hums a tune so sweet,
Echoed by the hearts it does greet.

Yet twilight beckons, shadows creep,
As memories weave and softly seep.
In every heart, the isle remains,
A song of joy, a thread of pains.

And when the stars begin to glow,
The last sigh calls us down below.
Together in the ocean's embrace,
We find our peace in this sacred place.

Through the Mists of Eternity

In the void where whispers dwell,
Time does spin its mystic spell.
Through the mists, we wander far,
Led by dreams and a silver star.

Each shadow dances, every light,
A tapestry of day and night.
With every step, the world unfurls,
A treasure trove of ancient pearls.

A sigh escapes the lips of fate,
Drifting softly, never late.
Moments lost and moments gained,
In the silence, we are chained.

Yet in the fog, we find the way,
Guided gently, come what may.
Through the labyrinth of the mind,
Truths entwined and joy defined.

So we traverse this endless path,
Embracing life, escaping wrath.
Through the mists, forever free,
We dance along eternity.

The Serpent's Lament at Twilight

In shadows deep where serpents glide,
A tale of woe cannot be denied.
Twilight drapes its velvet shawl,
And echoes haunt the ancient hall.

With jeweled eyes, it weaves its fate,
A song of sorrow, love, and hate.
Each hiss a whisper, soft and low,
A lament profound, a heart's bleak woe.

The fading light brings tales of yore,
Of battles fought on distant shore.
In solitude, the serpent weeps,
For dreams and hopes that darkness keeps.

Yet through the pain, a sliver shines,
A promise borne through tangled vines.
In twilight's glow, redemption's thread,
Awaits the serpent, hope not dead.

Under the stars, the lament fades,
A dance of shadows, the night parades.
With every breath, a chance to heal,
The serpent's heart begins to feel.

Fables of the Forgotten Grove

In the grove where whispers play,
Lost fables linger, night and day.
Leaves are pages, worn and wise,
Telling tales beneath the skies.

Ancient roots hold secrets deep,
Where memories of silence sleep.
Each breeze a story, gentle sway,
Of laughter shared in child's play.

With every turn, the shadows dance,
Enchanted nights invite a chance.
To wander far in realms unknown,
Where dreams are born, and seeds are sown.

Yet time is fleeting, soft and frail,
A fleeting breath, a potent tale.
In every corner, magic thrives,
Bringing forth the joy of lives.

So heed the grove's enchanting call,
Where echoes linger, one and all.
In its heart, the tales combine,
Fables woven, oh so divine.

Reflections on the Edge of Awareness

In the stillness where thoughts collide,
Quiet whispers from the deep abide.
Like a mirror, life reflects our yearn,
In the twilight, deeper truths we learn.

Glimmers dance along the water's skin,
Fleeting notions, where dreams begin.
In the heart of night, wisdom speaks clear,
Listen closely, for the answers are near.

Threads of time, they weave and entwine,
Each moment captured, a story divine.
Beneath the surface, secrets unfurl,
In the silence, magic starts to swirl.

A fleeting sigh, a breath of the past,
In the present, all shadows are cast.
Open your mind, let the wonders flow,
On the edge of awareness, let truth grow.

So step lightly, where the echoes play,
Each thought a treasure, fading away.
In the gentle embrace of the unknown,
We find ourselves, and we're never alone.

Curious Echoes from the Abyss

From the depths where shadows creep,
Curious whispers take the leap.
In the caverns where silence reigns,
The heart beats on, despite the chains.

A flicker of light, a spark of grace,
In the darkness, behold the face.
Reflections twisted, yet so profound,
What lost treasures in mirages found.

Ethereal voices call from afar,
Murmurs drifting like a fallen star.
With every echo, the past takes flight,
In the abyss, the soul ignites.

Silhouettes dance on the edge of fear,
What we seek might just draw near.
Embrace the darkness, let it unfold,
For within the abyss lies wisdom untold.

Step boldly forth from your safe retreat,
In the curious echoes, your heart will beat.
For the journey is rich, with wonder and dread,
And the abyss, my friend, is where dreams are fed.

The Solitude in an Enchanted Mist

When the morning breaks with a shrouded light,
Solitude wraps the world in soft white.
Each breath a tapestry, woven and spun,
In an enchanted mist, day's dance begun.

Whispers of nature, a gentle sigh,
Rustling leaves beneath a muted sky.
The magic of silence, a calming balm,
In solitude's hold, I find my calm.

Shadows linger where the sun peeks through,
In the mist, the ordinary feels new.
With every step, the enchantment grows,
In the stillness, the heart knows.

Glimmers of magic in droplets of dew,
A world transformed, the old made new.
In the embrace of the mist's soft kiss,
We find the elegance in moments of bliss.

So let us wander where the horizon blurs,
In this solitude, the soul ensures.
For in the enchanted mist we roam,
We discover the essence of our true home.

Shadows of the Moonlit Grove

In the grove where the moonlight spills,
Softly casting shadows, the night fulfills.
Whispers of trees in a language unknown,
Under the silver, we wander alone.

A path unwinds with secrets in tow,
Each step reveals where the wild things grow.
In the hush of the night, tales intertwine,
With every heartbeat, a story divine.

The fragrance of flowers, sweet in the air,
Drawing us deeper, a world rare.
Footsteps echo on the forest floor,
In the moonlit grove, we thirst for more.

Hiding in corners where dreams take flight,
Creatures of wonder dance with the night.
As shadows lengthen, the spirits arise,
Guiding our hearts beneath starlit skies.

So come, take my hand, let's drift in this place,
In the shadows, we're lost in embrace.
For the moonlit grove holds magic so near,
In its gentle arms, we shed our fear.

Ghostly Threads in the Driftwood Vale

In shadows deep where whispers play,
The driftwood sways, a ghostly sway.
Threads of mist weave through the trees,
A haunting song rides on the breeze.

Old tales spoken in muted tones,
Echo softly, like distant moans.
Each crumbled leaf tells stories old,
Of love and loss, both brave and bold.

In moonlit glades where shadows prance,
Lost spirits beckon for a chance.
Their silken strands twine through the night,
A dance of sorrow, lost from sight.

Yet hope ignites in the darkest shade,
A flicker soft that shan't soon fade.
For every ghost, a tale unfolds,
In driftwood vale, where time beholds.

Muffled Ripples Across the Lair's Edge

Muffled ripples touch the shore,
Whispers echo, tales of yore.
At the lair's edge, shadows blend,
Where secrets lie, the waters send.

Beneath the moon, the darkness flows,
In gentle curves, the magic grows.
Each breath a brush against the night,
A dreamlike realm, cloaked in twilight.

Silver fish dance in watery veils,
Chasing starlight, where magic trails.
In the deep, a soft charm sleeps,
As the world above softly weeps.

Across the surface, reflections play,
Drawing memories that drift away.
In the lair, whispers softly tease,
A silent promise upon the breeze.

Wistful Flows Through Reptilian Dreams

Through reptilian dreams, visions glide,
Where slow and steady worlds abide.
Waters swirl in gentle streams,
Carving paths through silent dreams.

Scales glitter in the morning light,
Each flicker a spark, a dance of might.
In sunlit pools, shadows play,
Tracing journeys that drift away.

In stillness lies a hidden song,
Ancient echoes where spirits throng.
Wistful flows guide the heart's pace,
In the depths, a pause, a space.

Yet dreams awaken with each new dawn,
As lizards bask on a carpeted lawn.
A world unfolds, both wild and grand,
In reptilian realms where magic stands.

Soft Glimmers on the Silken Fissure

Soft glimmers dance on silken strands,
A veil of wonder woven by hands.
Where twilight lingers, shadows feign,
A world awaits where dreams remain.

Each fiber tells a tale unheard,
A whispered secret, a fleeting word.
In the space between dark and light,
Soft glimmers spark, igniting the night.

Through silken fissures, echoes sway,
In delicate chambers, shadows play.
A realm where hope and sorrow meet,
Each heartbeat thrums with rhythmic beat.

As starlit threads weave tales anew,
In soft glimmers, a magical view.
The beauty lies beyond the seam,
In the gentle flow of a timeless dream.

Twilight's Gentle Embrace

In twilight's gentle, whispering sigh,
The stars awaken, one by one,
Casting their light on a world so shy,
As shadows dance 'neath the setting sun.

Soft colors mingle, a painter's dream,
A canvas bathed in lavender hues,
The horizon twinkles, a sparkling gleam,
As night enfolds in its velvet cues.

Creatures stir as the day gives way,
To nocturnal secrets hidden from light,
In this hushed embrace, the heart will sway,
Finding calm in the still of the night.

With every breeze, a sweet refrain,
A melody played on the whispers of air,
In twilight's arms, we feel no pain,
Just dreams taking flight, free from despair.

And when the moon reigns high above,
It fills the world with silvered grace,
Each twinkle a promise, a sign of love,
In twilight's gentle, warm embrace.

Secrets of the Faintly Glowing Lake

Beneath the stars, the water gleams,
A liquid mirror, soft and deep,
Where whispers weave through silken dreams,
And secrets hide in the depths of sleep.

The ripples tell of tales untold,
Of faeries dancing in moonlit guise,
In this haven, the brave and bold,
Can glimpse the truth behind their eyes.

Glistening reflections of past and lore,
Echo of laughter, sorrow, and grace,
A place where hearts may softly soar,
And memories linger in this sacred space.

As twilight lingers, the shadows play,
The mist embraces the fading light,
While nature hums its soft array,
In the tranquil arms of the night.

So come and wander along the shore,
To the faintly glowing lake's embrace,
Where every breath unveils more,
And every wave is a gentle trace.

Dreams Beneath the Silvered Sky

In night's tender arms, our dreams take flight,
Beneath a sky of shimmering stars,
Every wish, a glimmering light,
Guiding the heart through night's soft memoirs.

The moon, a guardian, draped in gold,
Watches over the secrets we share,
In whispered thoughts and stories bold,
She cradles our hopes with delicate care.

Clouds like cotton drift through the air,
As echoes of laughter weave through the night,
With every sigh, we shed our despair,
And revel in visions, ethereal and bright.

As starlight twinkles in a velvet sea,
We sail on dreams, unbound and free,
In the embrace of endless possibility,
Underneath this silvered canopy.

So close your eyes to the world outside,
Let your spirit soar on the winds of lore,
For in these dreams, our hearts abide,
And find their wings forevermore.

Navigating the Veil of Fog

In morning's blush, the fog drapes low,
A blanket thick, where whispers blend,
Through soft gray, paths seem to flow,
A mystery thick, no clear end.

With cautious steps, we tread the haze,
Every sound a call from the dim,
In this shroud, we lose the maze,
While shadows flicker, cold yet grim.

But in the silence, magic brews,
As ancient secrets unfurl their charms,
In every breath, the world renews,
And hidden wonders weave their arms.

We dance through dreams in this woven mist,
Where time unwinds like a silken thread,
Each heartbeat echoes a longing twist,
While hope ignites, a light ahead.

So trust the veil, let it guide your way,
For in the fog, the spirit can soar,
In every whisper, there's courage to stay,
Navigating the mist, we find so much more.

The Fading Echo of Time's Song

In shadows cast by ancient trees,
The whispers of the past still please.
A gentle breeze across the glen,
Calls forth the tales of long-gone men.

The clock ticks softly, time unwinds,
Memories linger, fate entwined.
A melody of forgotten dreams,
In twilight's glow, the silence gleams.

Each note, a heart that yearned to sing,
In echoes lost, the sorrows cling.
Yet in the dusk, a spark remains,
The fading song, eternal chains.

Embrace the dusk, yet hold the light,
For every end births another night.
In shadows deep, hope softly dwells,
In fading echoes, truth compels.

Whispers of the Forsaken Path

Upon the road where few have trod,
The air hangs thick, the silence awed.
A path once bright now cloaked in gray,
Whispers dance where shadows play.

Lost tales wander on the breeze,
Gentle sighs through dancing leaves.
Echoes of those who lost their way,
In the stillness, their spirits sway.

With every step, the heart now feels,
The weight of time, the truth it reveals.
Forsaken dreams that time forgot,
In twilight's grasp, their fate is caught.

Hold fast to threads of what was known,
For through the dark, seeds of light are sown.
The path may twist, but never ends,
In whispered tales, the journey bends.

When Reality Meets the Ethereal

When night descends and worlds collide,
The veil grows thin, the stars reside.
In shadows where the spirits dwell,
Reality and dreams conspire well.

A haunting light begins to glow,
Merging realms where few dare go.
In whispered tales of twilight's grace,
The ethereal finds its place.

Beyond the veil, the lost may find,
A glimpse of heart, a thread unkind.
When silence speaks, the truth emerges,
In depths below, the spirit surges.

So stand upon the edge of night,
Embrace the shadows, seek the light.
For in the blend of dreams and fate,
Lie mysteries we long await.

The Heartbeat of the Forgotten Dawn

At dawn's first light, a silence stirs,
The heartbeat echoes, softly purrs.
In hues of gold and longing gray,
The world awakens from its fray.

Forgotten dreams in morning's blush,
A gentle sigh, a tranquil hush.
The sun will rise, the shadows flee,
In every heart, a chance to be.

Awake the past, let memories flow,
Through woven threads of joy and woe.
In every pulse, a story lies,
Where hope anew forever ties.

So raise your gaze to skies aglow,
And feel the warmth, let heartbeats grow.
In every dawn, the chance to start,
The heartbeat sings within the heart.

Subdued Trajectories of the Ethereal Wing

In twilight's hush, the shadows play,
Where whispers dance and dreamers sway.
A gentle breath on feathered flight,
A tale unfolds beneath the night.

With stars as guides, they slip and slide,
Through realms where secrets dare to hide.
Each sigh a spell, each glance a thread,
Weaving the dreams where fears are shed.

In silence marked with mystic grace,
They soar above time and space.
With every beat of heart and wing,
The echoes of the past still sing.

So let the night keep watchful eyes,
Upon the paths where magic lies.
For in the dark, the light is found,
In whispers soft, the world is bound.

Listen close to the winds that weave,
A tapestry that none can grieve.
For in each fold, a story dwells,
Of life, of laughter, and of spells.

Faint Lullabies Beneath the Scaled Veil

In caverns deep where shadows flow,
A lullaby so soft and slow.
With scales that shimmer, deep and wide,
The echoes cradle dreams inside.

Beneath the veil, the whispers glide,
Where mysteries and fables bide.
A fragrance sweet, like cedar's breath,
Hints at tales of life and death.

Each note a wish, each pause a thread,
Of woven fables long since said.
In slumber's grasp, the world will bend,
To secrets only dreams can send.

With every rise of starlit skies,
The heartbeats pulse, like lullabies.
They drift through realms where shadows rest,
On wings of night, in dreams, we're blessed.

So close your eyes, let visions gleam,
In woven paths of silvered dream.
For in this dance of twilight hour,
We find the magic, we find the power.

Waning Currents of the Dragon's Grasp

In twilight's glow, the currents wane,
A dragon's grasp, both fierce and vain.
From craggy heights to valleys wide,
The echoes of their might abide.

With scales of gold, they soar the skies,
Their shadows cast, like whispered sighs.
In every flap, a thunder's roar,
Of legends lost on ancient shore.

Yet in their flight, a sorrow stirs,
A fading hope as silence purrs.
For every flame that lights the night,
A memory fades, lost from sight.

Beneath the moon's soft watchful gaze,
They chase the winds of former days.
And as they weave through starlit streams,
They hold the weight of whispered dreams.

So let them fly, let them embrace,
The waning fog, the lingering grace.
For in their wake, the world retains,
The songs of hearts and ancient chains.

Ethereal Resonance Along the Fabled Glide

Upon the winds of fabled dreams,
The echoes of the past still gleam.
In every turn, the stories weave,
Through realms where hope and magic leave.

Ethereal light guides every flight,
Where shadows dance in silvered night.
A tapestry of whispers wide,
In fleeting seconds, time will bide.

With every beat of fleeting wings,
The song of ages softly clings.
In currents swift, their spirits rise,
To trace the map of starlit skies.

So chase the winds with hearts aflame,
Let none forget the whispering name.
For in each glide, a promise sparks,
Of worlds reborn within the dark.

In silence held, the dreams persist,
Along the paths of twilight mist.
Where stories linger, hopes ignite,
Ethereal echoes take to flight.

www.ingramcontent.com/pod-product-compliance
Ingram Content Group UK Ltd.
Pitfield, Milton Keynes, MK11 3LW, UK
UKHW021503280125
4335UKWH00035B/678